Super Planner

Name: _____

Address: _____

City/State/Zip: _____

Phone: _____

Email: _____

Biz: _____

Biz Address: _____

Biz Phone: _____

Biz Email: _____

Design by April Chloe Terrazas
www.AprilChloeTerrazasAmazon.com
ISBN#: 978-1-941775-29-5

January	February	March	April	May	June
1_____	1_____	1_____	1_____	1_____	1_____
2_____	2_____	2_____	2_____	2_____	2_____
3_____	3_____	3_____	3_____	3_____	3_____
4_____	4_____	4_____	4_____	4_____	4_____
5_____	5_____	5_____	5_____	5_____	5_____
6_____	6_____	6_____	6_____	6_____	6_____
7_____	7_____	7_____	7_____	7_____	7_____
8_____	8_____	8_____	8_____	8_____	8_____
9_____	9_____	9_____	9_____	9_____	9_____
10_____	10_____	10_____	10_____	10_____	10_____
11_____	11_____	11_____	11_____	11_____	11_____
12_____	12_____	12_____	12_____	12_____	12_____
13_____	13_____	13_____	13_____	13_____	13_____
14_____	14_____	14_____	14_____	14_____	14_____
15_____	15_____	15_____	15_____	15_____	15_____
16_____	16_____	16_____	16_____	16_____	16_____
17_____	17_____	17_____	17_____	17_____	17_____
18_____	18_____	18_____	18_____	18_____	18_____
19_____	19_____	19_____	19_____	19_____	19_____
20_____	20_____	20_____	20_____	20_____	20_____
21_____	21_____	21_____	21_____	21_____	21_____
22_____	22_____	22_____	22_____	22_____	22_____
23_____	23_____	23_____	23_____	23_____	23_____
24_____	24_____	24_____	24_____	24_____	24_____
25_____	25_____	25_____	25_____	25_____	25_____
26_____	26_____	26_____	26_____	26_____	26_____
27_____	27_____	27_____	27_____	27_____	27_____
28_____	28_____	28_____	28_____	28_____	28_____
29_____	29_____	29_____	29_____	29_____	29_____
30_____		30_____	30_____	30_____	30_____
31_____		31_____	31_____	31_____	31_____

July	August	September	October	November	December
1 _____	1 _____	1 _____	1 _____	1 _____	1 _____
2 _____	2 _____	2 _____	2 _____	2 _____	2 _____
3 _____	3 _____	3 _____	3 _____	3 _____	3 _____
4 _____	4 _____	4 _____	4 _____	4 _____	4 _____
5 _____	5 _____	5 _____	5 _____	5 _____	5 _____
6 _____	6 _____	6 _____	6 _____	6 _____	6 _____
7 _____	7 _____	7 _____	7 _____	7 _____	7 _____
8 _____	8 _____	8 _____	8 _____	8 _____	8 _____
9 _____	9 _____	9 _____	9 _____	9 _____	9 _____
10 _____	10 _____	10 _____	10 _____	10 _____	10 _____
11 _____	11 _____	11 _____	11 _____	11 _____	11 _____
12 _____	12 _____	12 _____	12 _____	12 _____	12 _____
13 _____	13 _____	13 _____	13 _____	13 _____	13 _____
14 _____	14 _____	14 _____	14 _____	14 _____	14 _____
15 _____	15 _____	15 _____	15 _____	15 _____	15 _____
16 _____	16 _____	16 _____	16 _____	16 _____	16 _____
17 _____	17 _____	17 _____	17 _____	17 _____	17 _____
18 _____	18 _____	18 _____	18 _____	18 _____	18 _____
19 _____	19 _____	19 _____	19 _____	19 _____	19 _____
20 _____	20 _____	20 _____	20 _____	20 _____	20 _____
21 _____	21 _____	21 _____	21 _____	21 _____	21 _____
22 _____	22 _____	22 _____	22 _____	22 _____	22 _____
23 _____	23 _____	23 _____	23 _____	23 _____	23 _____
24 _____	24 _____	24 _____	24 _____	24 _____	24 _____
25 _____	25 _____	25 _____	25 _____	25 _____	25 _____
26 _____	26 _____	26 _____	26 _____	26 _____	26 _____
27 _____	27 _____	27 _____	27 _____	27 _____	27 _____
28 _____	28 _____	28 _____	28 _____	28 _____	28 _____
29 _____	29 _____	29 _____	29 _____	29 _____	29 _____
30 _____	30 _____	30 _____	30 _____	30 _____	30 _____
31 _____	31 _____	31 _____	31 _____	31 _____	31 _____

January	February	March

April	May	June

July	August	September

October	November	December

Awesome People

Awesome People

Week/Month: _____

___ Monday

___ Tuesday

___ Wednesday

___ Thursday

___ Friday

___Saturday/Sunday___

Goal Planning:

Projects:

To Do:

Week/Month: _____

___ Monday

___ Tuesday

___ Wednesday

___ Thursday

___ Friday

___ Saturday/Sunday___

Goal Planning:

Projects:

To Do:

Week/Month: _____

___ Monday	
___ Wednesday	
___ Friday	

___ Tuesday	
___ Thursday	
__Saturday/Sunday___	

Goal Planning:

Projects:

To Do:

Week/Month: _____

Monday	
___	_____

___ Monday

___ Tuesday

___ Wednesday

___ Thursday

___ Friday

___ Saturday/Sunday___

Goal Planning:

Projects:

To Do:

Week/Month: _____

___ Monday

___ Tuesday

___ Wednesday

___ Thursday

___ Friday

___Saturday/Sunday___

Goal Planning:

Projects:

To Do:

Week/Month: _____

___ **Monday**

___ **Tuesday**

___ **Wednesday**

___ **Thursday**

___ **Friday**

__ **Saturday**/**Sunday**___

Goal Planning:

Projects:

To Do:

Week/Month: _____

___ Monday

___ Tuesday

___ Wednesday

___ Thursday

___ Friday

___ Saturday/Sunday ___

Goal Planning:

Projects:

To Do:

___ Monday

_____
_____
_____
_____
_____
_____
_____
_____

___ Tuesday

_____
_____
_____
_____
_____
_____
_____
_____

___ Wednesday

_____
_____
_____
_____
_____
_____
_____
_____

___ Thursday

_____
_____
_____
_____
_____
_____
_____
_____

___ Friday

_____
_____
_____
_____
_____
_____
_____
_____

___Saturday/Sunday___

_____
_____
_____
_____
_____
_____
_____

Goal Planning:

Projects:

To Do:

___ Monday

___ Tuesday

___ Wednesday

___ Thursday

___ Friday

___Saturday/Sunday___

Goal Planning:

Projects:

To Do:

Week/Month: _____

___ Monday

___ Tuesday

___ Wednesday

___ Thursday

___ Friday

___ Saturday/Sunday___

Goal Planning:

Projects:

To Do:

___ Monday

___ Tuesday

___ Wednesday

___ Thursday

___ Friday

___Saturday/Sunday___

Goal Planning:

Projects:

To Do:

Week/Month: _____

___ Monday	_____
	_____
	_____
	_____
	_____
	_____

___ Tuesday	_____
	_____
	_____
	_____
	_____
	_____

___ Wednesday

___ Thursday

___ Friday

___Saturday/Sunday___

Goal Planning:

Projects:

To Do:

Week/Month: _____

___ Monday

___ Tuesday

___ Wednesday

___ Thursday

___ Friday

___Saturday/Sunday___

Goal Planning:

Projects:

To Do:

Week/Month: _____

_ Monday		_ Tuesday

_ Wednesday		_ Thursday

_ Friday		_Saturday/Sunday___

Goal Planning:

Projects:

To Do:

___ Monday

___ Tuesday

___ Wednesday

___ Thursday

___ Friday

___ Saturday/Sunday ___

Goal Planning:

Projects:

To Do:

__ Monday

__ Tuesday

__ Wednesday

__ Thursday

__ Friday

__ Saturday/Sunday___

Goal Planning:

Projects:

To Do:

Week/Month: _____

__ Monday	_____
__ Wednesday	_____
__ Friday	_____

__ Monday

_____
_____
_____
_____
_____
_____
_____

__ Tuesday

_____
_____
_____
_____
_____
_____
_____

__ Wednesday

_____
_____
_____
_____
_____
_____
_____

Thursday

_____
_____
_____
_____
_____
_____
_____

__ Friday

_____
_____
_____
_____
_____
_____
_____

__ Saturday/Sunday___

_____
_____
_____
_____
_____
_____
_____

Goal Planning:

Projects:

To Do:

Week/Month: _____

___ **Monday** _____
_____
_____
_____
_____
_____
_____

___ **Tuesday** _____
_____
_____
_____
_____
_____
_____
_____

___ **Wednesday** _____
_____
_____
_____
_____
_____
_____
_____

___ **Thursday** _____
_____
_____
_____
_____
_____
_____
_____

___ **Friday** _____
_____
_____
_____
_____
_____
_____

___ **Saturday/Sunday** ___ _____
_____
_____
_____
_____
_____

Goal Planning:

Projects:

To Do:

Week/Month: _____

____ Monday

____ Tuesday

____ Wednesday

____ Thursday

____ Friday

____Saturday/Sunday____

Goal Planning:

Projects:

To Do:

Week/Month: _____

___ Monday

___ Tuesday

___ Wednesday

___ Thursday

___ Friday

___Saturday/Sunday___

Goal Planning:

Projects:

To Do:

Week/Month: _____

___ Monday

Tuesday

___ Wednesday

Thursday

___ Friday

Saturday/Sunday___

Goal Planning:

Projects:

To Do:

___ Monday

___ Tuesday

___ Wednesday

___ Thursday

___ Friday

__Saturday/Sunday___

Goal Planning:

Projects:

To Do:

Week/Month: _____

___ Monday		___ Tuesday	

___ Monday

___ Tuesday

___ Wednesday

___ Thursday

___ Friday

___Saturday/Sunday___

Goal Planning:

Projects:

To Do:

___ Monday

___ Tuesday

___ Wednesday

___ Thursday

___ Friday

___ Saturday/Sunday___

Goal Planning:

Projects:

To Do:

Week/Month: _____

___ Monday

___ Tuesday

___ Wednesday

___ Thursday

___ Friday

___Saturday/Sunday___

Goal Planning:

Projects:

To Do:

Week/Month: _____

Monday _____

Tuesday _____

Wednesday _____

Thursday _____

Friday _____

Saturday/Sunday _____

Goal Planning:

Projects:

To Do:

Monday

___ _____
_____
_____
_____
_____
_____
_____

Tuesday

___ _____
_____
_____
_____
_____
_____
_____

Wednesday

___ _____
_____
_____
_____
_____
_____
_____

Thursday

___ _____
_____
_____
_____
_____
_____
_____

Friday

___ _____
_____
_____
_____
_____
_____
_____

Saturday/Sunday ___

_____
_____
_____
_____
_____
_____
_____

Goal Planning:

Projects:

To Do:

___ Monday

___ Tuesday

___ Wednesday

___ Thursday

___ Friday

___ Saturday/Sunday ___

Goal Planning:

Projects:

To Do:

___ Monday

___ Tuesday

___ Wednesday

___ Thursday

___ Friday

___Saturday/Sunday___

Goal Planning:

Projects:

To Do:

___ Monday

___ Tuesday

___ Wednesday

___ Thursday

___ Friday

___ Saturday/Sunday ___

Goal Planning:

Projects:

To Do:

Week/Month: _____

___ Monday

___ Tuesday

___ Wednesday

___ Thursday

___ Friday

___ Saturday/Sunday___

Goal Planning:

Projects:

To Do:

___ Monday

___ Tuesday

___ Wednesday

___ Thursday

___ Friday

___Saturday/Sunday___

Goal Planning:

Projects:

To Do:

Week/Month: _____

__ Monday

__ Tuesday

__ Wednesday

__ Thursday

__ Friday

__ Saturday/Sunday___

Goal Planning:

Projects:

To Do:

___ Monday

___ Tuesday

___ Wednesday

___ Thursday

___ Friday

___ Saturday/Sunday___

Goal Planning:

Projects:

To Do:

___ Monday

___ Tuesday

___ Wednesday

___ Thursday

___ Friday

__Saturday/Sunday____

Goal Planning:

Projects:

To Do:

Week/Month: _____

___ Monday

___ Tuesday

___ Wednesday

___ Thursday

___ Friday

___ Saturday/Sunday___

Goal Planning:

Projects:

To Do:

Week/Month: _____

____ Monday

____ Tuesday

____ Wednesday

____ Thursday

____ Friday

____Saturday/Sunday____

Goal Planning:

Projects:

To Do:

Week/Month: _____

| __ Monday | _____ |
| __ Tuesday | _____ |

__ Wednesday _____

__ Thursday _____

__ Friday _____

__Saturday/Sunday___ _____

Goal Planning:

Projects:

To Do:

___ Monday

___ Tuesday

___ Wednesday

___ Thursday

___ Friday

___ Saturday/Sunday___

Goal Planning:

Projects:

To Do:

Week/Month: _____

___ Monday	___ Tuesday

___ Wednesday	___ Thursday

___ Friday	___Saturday/Sunday___

Goal Planning:

Projects:

To Do:

Week/Month: _____

Monday
___

Tuesday
___

Wednesday
___

Thursday
___

Friday
___

__Saturday/Sunday___

Goal Planning:

Projects:

To Do:

Week/Month: _____

_____ Monday

Tuesday

_____ Wednesday

Thursday

_____ Friday

_____ Saturday/Sunday_____

Goal Planning:

Projects:

To Do:

Week/Month: _____

___ Monday		___ Tuesday	
	_____		_____
	_____		_____
	_____		_____
	_____		_____
	_____		_____
	_____		_____
	_____		_____
	_____		_____

___ Wednesday		___ Thursday	
	_____		_____
	_____		_____
	_____		_____
	_____		_____
	_____		_____
	_____		_____
	_____		_____

___ Friday		___Saturday/Sunday___	
	_____		_____
	_____		_____
	_____		_____
	_____		_____
	_____		_____
	_____		_____
	_____		_____

Goal Planning:

Projects:

To Do:

___ Monday

___ Tuesday

___ Wednesday

___ Thursday

___ Friday

___Saturday/Sunday___

Goal Planning:

Projects:

To Do:

___ Monday

___ Tuesday

___ Wednesday

___ Thursday

___ Friday

___ Saturday/Sunday___

Goal Planning:

Projects:

To Do:

___ Monday

___ Tuesday

___ Wednesday

___ Thursday

___ Friday

___Saturday/Sunday___

Goal Planning:

Projects:

To Do:

Week/Month: _____

Monday
_____

Tuesday
_____

Wednesday
_____

Thursday
_____

Friday
_____

Saturday/Sunday___

Goal Planning:

Projects:

To Do:

Week/Month: _____

___ Monday

___ Tuesday

___ Wednesday

___ Thursday

___ Friday

___ Saturday/Sunday___

Goal Planning:

Projects:

To Do:

Week/Month: _____

___ Monday

___ Tuesday

___ Wednesday

___ Thursday

___ Friday

___Saturday/Sunday___

Goal Planning:

Projects:

To Do:

Week/Month: _____

__ Monday	
__ Wednesday	
__ Friday	

__ Tuesday	
__ Thursday	
__Saturday/Sunday___	

Goal Planning:

Projects:

To Do:

___ Monday	_____	___ Tuesday	_____
	_____		_____
	_____		_____
	_____		_____
	_____		_____
	_____		_____
	_____		_____
	_____		_____

___ Wednesday	_____	___ Thursday	_____
	_____		_____
	_____		_____
	_____		_____
	_____		_____
	_____		_____
	_____		_____
	_____		_____

___ Friday	_____	___Saturday/Sunday___	_____
	_____		_____
	_____		_____
	_____		_____
	_____		_____
	_____		_____
	_____		_____

Goal Planning:

Projects:

To Do:

Week/Month: _____

___ Monday

___ Tuesday

___ Wednesday

___ Thursday

___ Friday

___ Saturday/Sunday ___

Goal Planning:

Projects:

To Do:

Week/Month: _____

___ Monday	_____	___ Tuesday	_____
	_____		_____
	_____		_____
	_____		_____
	_____		_____
	_____		_____
	_____		_____
	_____		_____

___ Wednesday	_____	___ Thursday	_____
	_____		_____
	_____		_____
	_____		_____
	_____		_____
	_____		_____
	_____		_____
	_____		_____

___ Friday	_____	___Saturday/Sunday___	_____
	_____		_____
	_____		_____
	_____		_____
	_____		_____
	_____		_____
	_____		_____

Goal Planning:

Projects:

To Do:

___ Monday

___ Tuesday

___ Wednesday

___ Thursday

___ Friday

___ Saturday/Sunday ___

Goal Planning:

Projects:

To Do:

Week/Month: _____

___ Monday

___ Tuesday

___ Wednesday

___ Thursday

___ Friday

___ Saturday/Sunday___

Goal Planning:

Projects:

To Do:

Week/Month: _____

Monday	
	_____
	_____
	_____
	_____
	_____
	_____
	_____

Tuesday	
	_____
	_____
	_____
	_____
	_____
	_____
	_____

Wednesday	
	_____
	_____
	_____
	_____
	_____
	_____
	_____

Thursday	
	_____
	_____
	_____
	_____
	_____
	_____
	_____

Friday	
	_____
	_____
	_____
	_____
	_____
	_____
	_____

Saturday/Sunday___	
	_____
	_____
	_____
	_____
	_____
	_____
	_____

Goal Planning:

Projects:

To Do:

___ Monday

___ Tuesday

___ Wednesday

___ Thursday

___ Friday

___ Saturday/Sunday___

Goal Planning:

Projects:

To Do:

Week/Month: _____

___ Monday

___ Tuesday

___ Wednesday

___ Thursday

___ Friday

___ Saturday/Sunday ___

Goal Planning:

Projects:

To Do:

April Chloe Terrazas is having a blast as an educator, writer, photographer and entrepreneur in Austin, Texas. She graduated from The University of Texas at Austin, College of Natural Sciences with a Bachelor's in Science specializing in Human Biology and is a Life Member of the Texas Exes Alumni Association and the Texas Exes Hispanic Alumni Committee.

As a freshman at UT, she established a private tutoring service. She has been a teacher and tutor for all ages from pre-kindergarten through college, specializing in mathematics and science.

She is the creator of The Complementary Method--a classroom platform for empowerment, kindness and anti-bullying. This Method is absolutely free to all educators and comes in a printable email packet for the entire school year. The Complementary Method is designed to bring students together to work as a team, to be good friends, to empower each other and to respect their teacher. All students should help each other become better together, not just a few excelling and others being left behind.

April owns Crazy Brainz Publishing where she is a math, science and family author and illustrator. She incorporates candy colored illustrations with math and science, bringing a new perspective to the field and making it enjoyable for all ages!

All of her titles are available at Amazon.com and BN.com.
(www.AprilChloeTerrazasAmazon.com for her Author Page).

She has toured the United States (Texas, California, Florida, New York, and Massachusetts) presenting science discussions to elementary schools and along the way she donates books to schools and families in need worldwide. She is currently available for science presentation bookings in the US, Canada, Caribbean, UK and Europe. April can be contacted through her website, Crazy-Brainz.com. Low income schools are eligible for book donations, also contact through the website.

Additionally, April has worked as a family, portrait and pet photographer in Austin, Texas since 2007. Anyone who knows her knows she loves animals more than anything. At some point, don't be surprised if you see her opening her own Animal Sanctuary!

In her spare time, April enjoys volunteering at local schools, helping students in need with math, science, reading and writing.

If you enjoyed this planner, please tell us so with a 5-STAR REVIEW @
www.AprilChloeTerrazasAmazon.com!

Check out the new
**CONFERENCE
PLANNERS**
now available online!

www.ingramcontent.com/pod-product-compliance
Lightning Source LLC
Chambersburg PA
CBHW040312050426
42452CB00018B/2809